Comfort for a Child's Heart

The 23rd Psalm and Bible Promises

written by Helen Haidle

illustrated by David Haidle

COMFORT FOR A CHILD'S HEART
published by Gold 'n' Honey Books
a division of Multnomah Publishers, Inc.

© 1999 by Multnomah Publishers, Inc.
Illustrations © 1999 by David Haidle
International Standard Book Number 1-57673-569-9

Design by David Haidle
Cover design by Mark Mickel

Gold 'n' Honey is a trademark of Multnomah Publishers, Inc.,
and is registered in the U.S. Patent and Trademark Office.

Scripture quotations are from: *The Holy Bible*, New King James Version (NKJV)
© 1984 by Thomas Nelson, Inc. unless otherwise noted.

Also quoted:
The Holy Bible, New International Version (NIV) © 1973, 1984 by International Bible
Society, used by permission of Zondervan Publishing House

Revised Standard Version Bible (RSV) © 1946, 1952 by the Division of
Christian Education of the National Council of the Churches of Christ
in the United States of America

The Good News Bible: The Bible in Today's English Version (TEV)
© 1976 by American Bible Society

The Living Bible (TLB)
© 1971. Used by permission of Tyndale House Publishers, Inc.
All rights reserved.

Printed in Hong Kong

ALL RIGHTS RESERVED
No part of this publication may be reproduced, stored in a retrieval system,
or transmitted, in any form or by any means—electronic, mechanical,
photocopying, recording, or otherwise—without prior written permission.

For information:
MULTNOMAH PUBLISHERS, INC.
POST OFFICE BOX 1720
SISTERS, OREGON 97759

99 00 01 02 03 04 — 10 9 8 7 6 5 4 3 2 1

To Pastor Ron Mehl,
a faithful shepherd in Beaverton, Oregon.
You have fed us God's Word and
led us in the worship of our Good Shepherd.
We praise God for your ministry.

To Don Goodman,
Editor Extraordinaire.
Your touch has blessed this book...and us!

And to Bernie Bradley,
gingerbread-boy-maker, seamstress, friend.
You've blessed us in many ways,
and you planted the seed for this book.

The 23rd Psalm

The Lord is my shepherd;
I shall not want.
He makes me to lie down in green pastures;
He leads me beside the still waters.
He restores my soul;
He leads me in the paths of righteousness
For His name's sake.
Yea, though I walk through
the valley of the shadow of death,
I will fear no evil;
For You are with me;
Your rod and Your staff, they comfort me.
You prepare a table before me
in the presence of my enemies;
You anoint my head with oil;
My cup runs over.
Surely goodness and mercy shall follow me
All the days of my life;
And I will dwell
in the house of the Lord forever.

Comfort for a Child's Heart

King David, one of the greatest kings in the land of Israel, wrote this Psalm. As a young man he had spent many years tending sheep in the fields around Bethlehem. He may have sung this to his flock.

David saw that people were like sheep and the Lord God was like a shepherd. When David wrote this Psalm, he talked about himself as a sheep. And he called the Lord his shepherd.

Hundreds of years later, Jesus lived on the earth. Jesus said He was the Good Shepherd who was willing to die for His sheep. Jesus proved it by giving His life for us. And God raised Him from the dead. Now Jesus can be your Good Shepherd, today and forever.

"The Lord is my shepherd."

Who is the Lord? The Lord is the One who made our universe, which overflows with stars and planets, apples and butterflies, owls and lions. This same Lord made *you* and knows all about you!

Who is a shepherd? A shepherd is one who watches over sheep and takes care of them—their food, their water, their safety, and their health. The shepherd never takes time off. His helpless sheep need him always.

The *best* shepherd of all is Jesus. He is the Good Shepherd because He gave His life for you.

Jesus loves you and cares for you just as a shepherd cares for one of his lambs. Jesus loves you so much He even knows your name. He wants to be *your* shepherd.

Sheep know the sound of their shepherd's voice. They follow no one but their shepherd. Just like a sheep, you can learn to know and trust Jesus as your Good Shepherd. And you can follow Him and do what He tells you.

Ask Yourself

Do you trust Jesus as your Lord and Shepherd?

How often do you take time to be close to Jesus through prayer and reading the Bible?

Get to know Him! You are one of His precious lambs.

The Lord Is My Shepherd

Jesus said, "I am the good shepherd. The good shepherd gives his life for the sheep. But a hireling, he who is not the shepherd, one who does not own the sheep, sees the wolf coming and leaves the sheep and flees; and the wolf catches the sheep and scatters them.

"The hireling flees because he...does not care about the sheep. I am the good shepherd; and I know My sheep...and I lay down My life for the sheep."

John 10:11–15

Share with Your Family

Make a Memory Box. Fill an old recipe box with 3x5 cards. Write this chapter's Memory Verse on the first card. Read your verse out loud at mealtimes each day until you have it memorized. Use a new card for each memory verse.

What did Jesus do to show that He was a *good* shepherd? Why do you need Him as your shepherd?

How can you follow Jesus, as lambs follow their shepherd?

How do you hear His voice?

Bible Promises

Jesus said, "My sheep...shall never perish;
neither shall anyone snatch them out of My hand."
John 10:27–28

"The Lord God...will feed His flock like a shepherd;
He will gather the lambs with His arm,
And carry them in His bosom."
Isaiah 40:10–11

"And when the Chief Shepherd [Jesus] appears,
you will receive the crown of glory that does not fade away."
1 Peter 5:4

"Now may the God of peace who brought up our Lord Jesus
from the dead, that great Shepherd of the sheep,
...make you complete...to do His will."
Hebrews 13:20–21

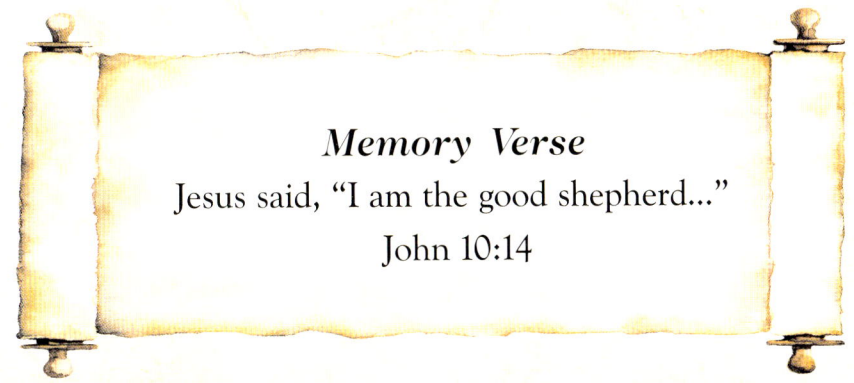

Memory Verse
Jesus said, "I am the good shepherd..."
John 10:14

"I shall not want."

"I shall not want" means I shall not be *in* want. The sheep will lack nothing. They may not have everything they *want* during a long, cold winter. But their shepherd will make sure they have everything they *need*.

What do sheep need? A shelter, water, and food. The sheep cannot take care of themselves. They must count on their shepherd to bring them water to drink and dry food to eat. And He must find a place to live.

During tough times, the sheep stay happy as long as they trust their good shepherd to give them what they need.

Like a good shepherd, Jesus stays close to you during problems and tough times. He loves you and He wants you to trust Him to take care of you. No problem is too big for Him.

Jesus promises to give you everything you need. Most of all, you need Jesus!

Ask Yourself

Are you satisfied with what Jesus gives you? Or do you gripe about what you *don't* have?

"I shall not want" doesn't mean that you shouldn't *want* something. It means that you can trust Jesus to know what you need.

Be willing to trust Jesus even when you don't have everything you *want*.

I Shall Not Want

Jesus' disciples told Him, "...Send the multitudes away, that they may go...buy themselves food."

Jesus said, "...You give them something to eat."

They said, "We have...only five loaves and two fish...."

"[Jesus] said, 'Bring them here to Me.' He commanded the multitudes to sit down on the grass. And He took the five loaves and the two fish, and... He blessed and broke and gave the loaves to the disciples; and the disciples gave to the multitudes. So they all ate and were filled, and they took up twelve baskets full of the fragments that remained. Now those who had eaten were about five thousand men, besides women and children." Matthew 14:15–21

Share with Your Family

Walk outdoors together. Watch the birds and find some wildflowers.

What can you learn from birds and flowers?

What are your three biggest worries?

Why is it so easy to worry when things go wrong? Is anything too difficult for Jesus?

What do you *need*? How does the story of the feeding of the 5,000 help you trust Jesus today?

Bible Promises

"For with God nothing will be impossible."
Luke 1:37

"Leave all your worries with him, because he cares for you."
1 Peter 5:7 (TEV)

Jesus said, "I am with you always, even to the end of the age."
Matthew 28:20

Jesus said, "Do not worry about your life,
what you will eat or what you will drink;
nor about your body, what you will put on…"
Matthew 6:25

"Delight yourself also in the Lord, and
He shall give you the desires of your heart."
Psalm 37:4

Memory Verse

"And my God shall supply all your need
according to His riches in glory by Christ Jesus."
Philippians 4:19

"He makes me to lie down in green pastures."

Sheep need plenty of good food. They usually graze from dawn until midmorning. A shepherd leads them to green pastures, which they cannot find on their own. Then he leads them to new pastures; otherwise, they would eat the grass down to the bare ground.

Once the sheep eat their fill, they must lie down and chew their cud. If one sheep bullies or butts another, this upsets all the sheep. They will refuse to lie down. Then their food cannot digest. They soon lose weight and grow weak. The shepherd stops the fighting at once and the sheep lie down to chew their cud.

Just as a shepherd calms his flock when he sits down among them, Jesus calms you with His peace. He does not want you to feel upset. When you go to bed at night, He will help you relax and sleep. Think about Jesus, not about your worries.

Ask Yourself

When you feel upset, do you talk to Jesus? Do you ask Him to calm your heart?

When you feel afraid or can't fall asleep, will you trust Jesus?

Do you receive peace by reading God's Word?

Jesus wants you to give Him your worries and fears. Pray to Him when others upset you or fight with you. Jesus is close by. He is your peace.

He Makes Me to Lie Down in Green Pastures

Jesus said, "Let not your heart be troubled; you believe in God, believe also in Me...Peace I leave with you, My peace I give to you; not as the world gives do I give to you. Let not your heart be troubled, neither let it be afraid." John 14:1, 27

On Easter Sunday evening after His resurrection from the dead, "Jesus came and stood in the midst, and said to [His disciples], 'Peace be with you.'" John 20:19

Share with Your Family

Lie on a rug, turn off the lights, and play a tape or CD of peaceful music.

How much would it be worth to you to have peace in your home? your school? the world?

What upsets you and takes away your peace?

How can Jesus give you peace when you feel upset or afraid?

What would you tell someone who felt upset and worried?

Bible Promises

"I will both lie down in peace, and sleep;
For You alone, O Lord, make me dwell in safety."
Psalm 4:8

"...and the peace of God...will guard your hearts and
minds through Christ Jesus."
Philippians 4:7

"You will keep him in perfect peace, whose mind
is stayed on You, because he trusts in You."
Isaiah 26:3

"The Lord bless you and keep you;
The Lord make His face shine upon you,...
And give you peace."
Numbers 6:24–26

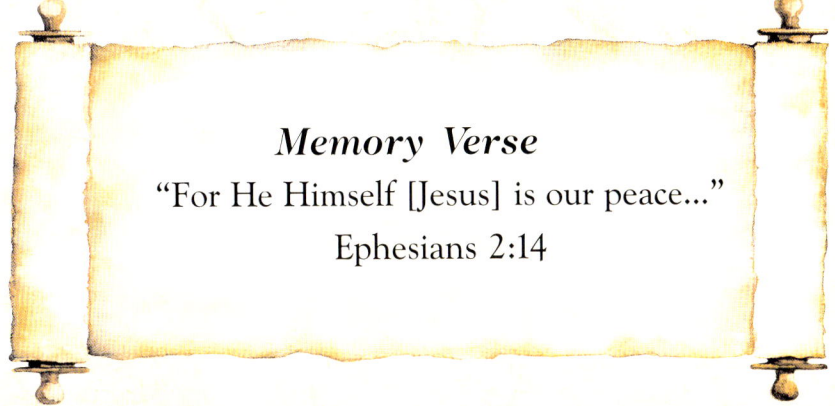

Memory Verse
"For He Himself [Jesus] is our peace..."
Ephesians 2:14

"He leads me beside the still waters."

Sheep need to drink lots of water. Their bodies are made up of 70 percent water. When they feel thirsty, they drink any water they find.

Sheep do not know the dangers of drinking in the muddy puddles along the road. This water is dusty and moldy. Other flocks walk through it and use it for their bathroom.

When sheep drink this water, some of them become sick and some of them die. Sheep cannot tell the difference between clean water and dirty water, so their shepherd finds clean water for them.

The water must also be still and quiet or the sheep will not drink it. Brooks and streams make noise that frightens the sheep. Sometimes a shepherd must dig a ditch to make a pool of water from which the sheep can drink in peace.

Jesus promised living water to everyone whose heart thirsts for God. If you go your own way, your thirst will lead you to dirty waters. You'll make choices that can hurt you. Jesus gives you living water and helps you make the best choices.

Ask Yourself

Are you *thirsty* to know Jesus better?

Do you want to please Jesus and do what's right?

How do you let Jesus help you know what to do? Your Good Shepherd knows what's best for you. He alone satisfies your *thirst*.

He Leads Me beside the Still Waters

Once Jesus told a woman by a well, "Whoever drinks of this water will thirst again, but whoever drinks of the water that I shall give him will never thirst. But the water that I shall give him will become in him a fountain of water springing up into everlasting life." John 4:13–14

Jesus told people who were gathered at a feast, "If anyone thirsts, let him come to Me and drink. He who believes in Me...out of his heart will flow rivers of living water." John 7:37–38

Share with Your Family

Eat salty pretzels or chips. Set out a glass pitcher of cool water, but serve it only after you discuss these questions:

How does it feel to be very thirsty?

What did Jesus mean when He said He would give us water so we will never thirst?

Have you ever received a gift you wanted for a long time, only to find it wasn't as great as you thought? How did you feel? Can you find true happiness without Jesus?

Bible Promises

"As the deer pants for the water brooks, so pants my soul for You, O God. My soul thirsts for God, for the living God." Psalm 42:1–2

"For I will pour water upon him that is thirsty, and floods on the dry ground: I will pour My Spirit on your descendants, and My blessings on your offspring." Isaiah 44:3

"For [Jesus] who is in the midst of the throne will shepherd them and lead them to living fountains of waters." Revelation 7:17

"Blessed are they which do hunger and thirst for righteousness, for they shall be filled." Matthew 5:6

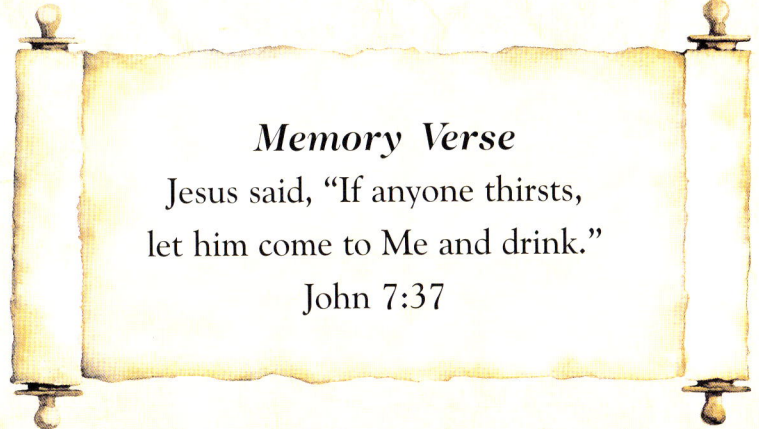

Memory Verse
Jesus said, "If anyone thirsts, let him come to Me and drink."
John 7:37

"He restores my soul."

A thick coat of wool makes sheep top-heavy. They easily lose their balance as they climb rocky hillsides in search of food. The sheep topple over onto their backs, like turtles.

An upside-down sheep cannot turn over by itself. It frantically waves its legs in the air until it wears itself out. If the sun beats down on its belly, the sheep may die within several hours.

A good shepherd keeps close watch over his sheep. Whenever he discovers one missing, he searches for it right away. He wants to *restore* it— to save it and bring it back to the safety of the flock.

Once the shepherd finds his lost sheep, he turns it over and rubs its legs to start the flow of blood. Knowing the legs are weak, he lifts the sheep onto his shoulders and carries it home. He is not angry. He is happy to find his lost sheep.

Jesus was never angry at people who were in trouble and asked for help. He said that He came to seek and to save those who had fallen away from God and were *lost*.

Ask Yourself

When have you been in trouble and needed help?

Do you ever wonder if Jesus feels angry when you've messed up?

Do you believe that when you ask Him to forgive you, He does? Remember that Jesus, your good shepherd, will love you and carry you when you're weak.

He Restores My Soul

"Then all the...sinners drew near to [Jesus] to hear Him. And the Pharisees...complained, saying, 'This Man receives sinners and eats with them.'"

[Jesus said,] "What man of you, having a hundred sheep, if he loses one of them, does not leave the ninety-nine in the wilderness, and go after the one which is lost until he finds it? And when he has found it, he lays it on his shoulders, rejoicing.

"And when he comes home, he calls together his friends...'Rejoice with me, for I have found my sheep which was lost!'" Luke 15:1–2, 4–6

Share with Your Family

Get out an item you'd recently lost or misplaced. Climb together onto one family member's bed to read and talk about this chapter.

When have you found something you lost? How did you feel while it was lost? How did you feel when you found it?

Have you ever felt like a lost sheep?

Talk about a time when you were in trouble and you needed help. What happened?

Kneel and pray for people who are "lost sheep."

Bible Promises

"As a shepherd seeks out his flock...so will I seek out
My sheep...from all the places where they were scattered."
Ezekiel 34:12

"If I say, 'My foot slips,' Your mercy, O Lord,
will hold me up." Psalm 94:18

"Create in me a clean heart, O God...
Restore to me the joy of Your salvation,
And uphold me by Your generous Spirit."
Psalm 51:10, 12

"Those who wait on the Lord shall renew their strength;
They shall mount up with wings like eagles,
They shall run and not be weary...and not faint."
Isaiah 40:31

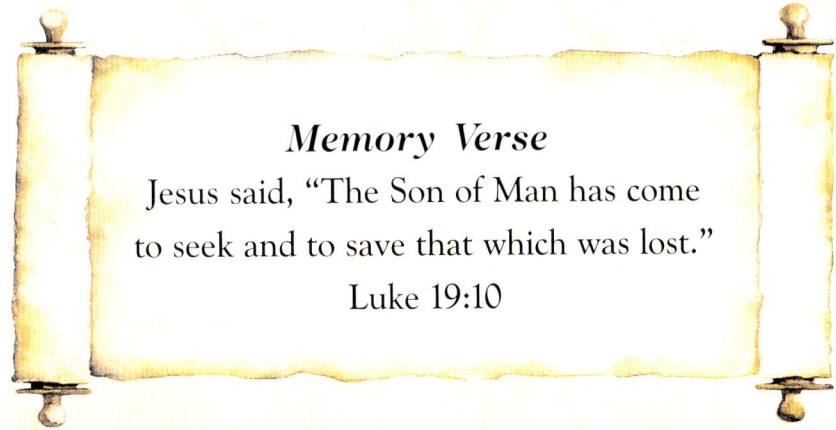

Memory Verse
Jesus said, "The Son of Man has come
to seek and to save that which was lost."
Luke 19:10

"He leads me in the paths of righteousness for His Name's sake."

No creatures lose their way more easily than sheep. Without a shepherd, sheep wander in the wrong direction, trot off the main paths, and never find their way back home.

A shepherd knows the best places for his sheep to feed safely. They must trust him and follow him to new pastures.

Sometimes a sheep goes its own way. The shepherd brings the stray sheep back onto the right path. He knows the sheep's own choices usually lead to danger or death.

Stubborn sheep that go their own way miss out on the shepherd's best plans for them. People, like sheep, make wrong choices too.

Jesus is the Good Shepherd who says, *"Follow Me."* He alone knows the right path for your life. Every person must make a decision to follow Jesus or risk going his or her own way.

Ask Yourself

Do you insist on doing what *you* want, even when it's wrong?

Going your own way may land you in trouble. Don't stray from God's path of doing right.

Choices are important—whether to obey your parents, to do your work well, to be fair, to love others. Will you choose what pleases yourself or what pleases your Good Shepherd?

He Leads Me in the Paths of Righteousness

Jesus said, "Enter by the narrow gate; for wide is the gate and broad is the way that leads to destruction, and there are many who go in by it.

"Because narrow is the gate and difficult is the way which leads to life, and there are few who find it." Matthew 7:13–14

Jesus said, "And where I go you know, and the way you know....I am the way, the truth, and the life. No one comes to the Father except through Me."
John 14:4, 6

Share with Your Family

Play "Follow the Leader" through your house and out into the yard. Take turns being the leader.

Did you enjoy following someone else? Which would you rather be—a leader or a follower?

When have you found it difficult to follow Jesus? What happened?

What's the difference between following Jesus and going your own way?

When have you made choices to follow Jesus? How will you follow Him today?

Bible Promises

"All we like sheep have gone astray;
We have turned, every one, to his own way;
And the Lord has laid on [Jesus] the iniquity of us all."
Isaiah 53:6

"I will instruct you and
teach you in the way you should go."
Psalm 32:8

Jesus said, "My sheep...follow Me. And I give them eternal life, and they shall never perish; neither shall anyone snatch them out of My hand." John 10:27–28

"For this is God, our God forever and ever;
He will be our guide even to death."
Psalm 48:14

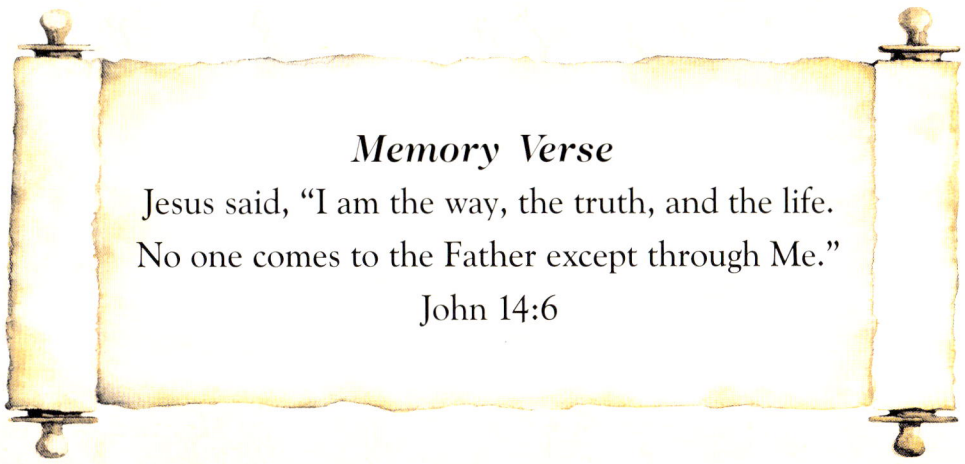

Memory Verse
Jesus said, "I am the way, the truth, and the life.
No one comes to the Father except through Me."
John 14:6

"Yea, though I walk through the
valley of the shadow of death,
I will fear no evil;
For You are with me."

There is a Valley of the Shadow of Death in the land of Israel. The four-mile long valley wall rises hundreds of feet in some places. Wolves, wild dogs, and snakes hide in this valley. This is the most dangerous part of the journey on the way to the best highland pastures.

Sometimes the path is too narrow for a sheep to turn around. Sometimes a wide gully cuts part of the path in half. Sheep must jump across the gap to follow their shepherd!

Sheep never walk through this dark valley alone if they stay close to their shepherd. He knows the way. He has been there before.

Jesus experienced pain, suffering, and trouble, even death on a cross. He understands how you feel. He knows everything you face. And He is with you, no matter what happens!

Ask Yourself

What frightens you the most?

What do you do when you feel frightened?

Do you ever fear events that haven't even happened?

Don't be afraid. No dark valley or trouble can ever separate you from Jesus, not even death. Remember, Jesus went *through* the valley of the shadow of death and came out alive!

Though I Walk through the Valley of the Shadow of Death, I Will Fear No Evil; For You Are with Me

Friday afternoon on the cross "...when Jesus had cried out with a loud voice, He said, 'Father, into Your hands I commit My spirit.'" Luke 23:46

Early Sunday morning, women came to the grave and an angel told them, "Do not be afraid, for I know that you seek Jesus who was crucified. He is not here; for He is risen, as He said. Come, see the place where the Lord lay. And go quickly and tell His disciples that He is risen from the dead." Matthew 28:5–7

Share with Your Family

Select a difficult job around the house or yard. Have the whole family work on it together.

Discuss some of the hardest times your family has experienced. How has Jesus helped you go through the *dark valleys?* What do you face right now?

Read how Jesus walked through the valley of the shadow of death in Matthew 27:27—28:10.

How does knowing that Jesus died and rose from the dead encourage you?

Bible Promises

"For I, the Lord your God, will hold your right
hand, saying to you, 'Fear not, I will help you.'"
Isaiah 41:13

"For You are my lamp, O Lord;
The Lord shall enlighten my darkness."
2 Samuel 22:29

Jesus said, "In this world you will have trouble.
But take heart! I have overcome the world."
John 16:33 (NIV)

"Fear not,...I have called you by your name;
You are Mine. When you pass through the waters,
I will be with you."
Isaiah 43:1-2

Memory Verse

"The Lord will deliver me from every evil work."
2 Timothy 4:18

"Your rod and Your staff, they comfort me."

A shepherd takes pride in his rod and his staff. He finds the best kinds of wood. Then he carves them to fit his hand.

The rod is like a club. The shepherd uses it mainly as a weapon to defend the flock. For hours he practices throwing it. When wolves or lions attack the sheep, the shepherd throws his rod at them. One hard blow on the head sends them running.

The shepherd's staff is a long walking stick. The shepherd guides a sheep by pressing his staff against its side. With the curved end he can hook a sheep's leg to pull it away from the edge of a cliff.

To show his love, the shepherd gently strokes a sheep's side with his staff. Sometimes he uses it to urge a shy lamb to walk closer to him.

The rod and the staff *comfort* the sheep and help them feel safe and happy. Jesus uses God's Word, the Bible, like a rod and a staff to guide you and remind you of His love. Jesus also sends the Holy Spirit to be your Comforter.

Ask Yourself

How has God's Word given you joy and comfort?

Do you memorize God's Word? It is more powerful than any rod. It will help build your faith!

Does the cross of Jesus comfort you, as the shepherd's staff comforts the sheep? It should—the cross reminds you that Jesus gave His life for you.

Your Rod and Your Staff, They Comfort Me

Jesus said, "And I will pray the Father, and He will give you another Helper [Comforter], that He may abide with you forever—the Spirit of truth...you know Him, for He dwells with you and will be in you." John 14:16–17

"The Helper [Comforter], the Holy Spirit, whom the Father will send in My name, He will teach you all things, and bring to your remembrance all things that I said to you." John 14:26

Share with Your Family

Cuddle under a warm comforter (or a blanket) in the coziest place in your house and eat some "comfort" food while you read this chapter.

How has Jesus' love encouraged your family?
How do you need the Holy Spirit's comfort?
How does Jesus say the Holy Spirit will help you today?
Do you know someone that needs encouragement and comfort? What could you do to help?

Bible Promises

"As one whom his mother comforts, so I will comfort you; and you shall be comforted."
Isaiah 66:13

"Praise be the...God of all comfort, who comforts us in all our troubles, so that we can comfort those in any trouble with the comfort we ourselves have received from God."
2 Corinthians 1:3–4 (NIV)

"Wait for the Lord; be strong and take heart and wait for the Lord."
Psalm 27:14 (NIV)

"Blessed are those who mourn,
For they shall be comforted."
Matthew 5:4

Memory Verse

"While we were still weak, at the right time Christ died for [us]."
Romans 5:6 (RSV)

"You prepare a table before me in the presence of my enemies."

We usually eat from a table. High flat places of mountain sheep ranges are called "tables." These are the very best pastures. The shepherd "prepares" the table for his flock by scouting out its enemies: wild animals and poisonous plants.

Sheep cannot tell the difference between poisonous and nonpoisonous plants. One nibble of the white camas flower will kill a lamb. The shepherd finds and destroys all poisonous plants so his flock can feed safely. He works hard to protect them.

Jesus does more to feed you and protect you from your enemies than any earthly shepherd ever does to feed and protect his flock. Jesus gave His life so you could live forever as part of God's heavenly family.

"I am the bread of life," said Jesus. When you believe in Him, He fills a hunger in your heart that only He can satisfy. And you can be sure He has already prepared a *feast* for you in heaven.

Ask Yourself

Do you trust in Jesus to be your "bread"...to fill you and make you happy?

Imagine what it will be like to *dine* with Jesus in heaven. He is preparing a banquet for you, one of His honored guests.

You Prepare a Table before Me in the Presence of My Enemies

Jesus said, "My Father gives you the true bread from heaven. For the bread of God is He who comes down from heaven and gives life to the world."

The people said, "Lord, give us this bread always."

Jesus said, "I am the bread of life. He who comes to Me shall never hunger...I am the living bread which came down from heaven. If anyone eats of this bread, he will live forever; and the bread that I shall give is My flesh, which I shall give for the life of the world." John 6:32–35, 51

Share with Your Family

Bake or buy a loaf of unsliced bread. Sit together on a blanket outdoors or in your living room. Pull off chunks of bread and eat.

Why is bread important? Why do you think Jesus called Himself the "bread of life"?

Can you remember people in the Bible who were fed? (Exodus 16:11–17, 1 Kings 17:1–7, John 6:1–14)

In what ways does Jesus feed you?

Bible Promises

Jesus said, "I am the living bread...
If anyone eats of this bread, he will live forever..."
John 6:51

"Behold, I stand at the door and knock. If anyone hears
My voice and opens the door, I will come in to him and
dine with him, and he with Me."
Revelation 3:20

Jesus told Peter, "Feed My lambs...Feed My sheep."
John 21:15, 17

"The Lord Jesus, on the night he was betrayed, took
bread, and when he had given thanks, he broke it and said,
'This is my body, which is for you.'"
1 Corinthians 11:23–24 (NIV)

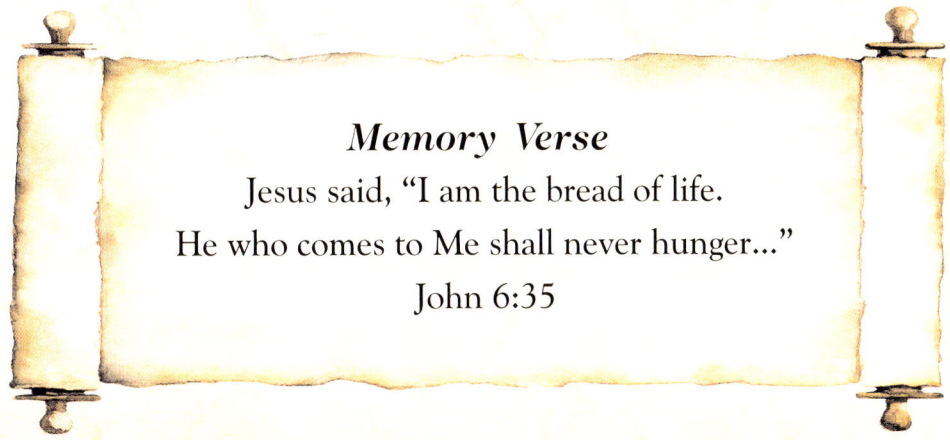

Memory Verse
Jesus said, "I am the bread of life.
He who comes to Me shall never hunger..."
John 6:35

"You anoint my head with oil."

Every day, the shepherd looks over his sheep for cuts and scrapes. Wounds from thorns and sharp rocks can cause infection. Every shepherd owns a large bowl of soothing olive oil that he pours over all the wounds. This pouring of oil is called anointing.

The shepherd also anoints his sheep to protect them from nasal flies. The flies land on a sheep's nose and lay their eggs. The eggs hatch into tiny worms that burrow up the sheep's nose into its head.

The wriggling worms cause the sheep to panic. It tosses its head and runs wild. Trying to rid itself of the pain, the sheep beats its head against a rock or a tree, often hurting itself.

At the first sight of nasal flies, the shepherd rubs a mixture of oil and herbs over every sheep's head and nose. This keeps the flies away and calms the sheep.

Just as oil calms the sheep, Jesus wants to calm our upset minds and hearts with the Holy Spirit.

Ask Yourself

What upsets you? What frustrates you and causes you to panic?

Who irritates or "bugs" you?

When things go wrong and upset you, ask Jesus to anoint you with His love and peace. Pray for the Holy Spirit to take control of your life.

You Anoint My Head with Oil

After His baptism, Jesus "...being filled with the Holy Spirit, returned from the Jordan and was led by the Spirit into the wilderness."   Luke 4:1

After being tempted in the wilderness "Jesus returned in the power of the Spirit..."   Luke 4:14

Later Jesus read out loud from the book of Isaiah: "The Spirit of the Lord is upon Me..."   Luke 4:18

"When [the disciples] had prayed,...they were all filled with the Holy Spirit, and they spoke the word of God with boldness...with great power [they] gave witness...And great grace was upon them all."
    Acts 4:31, 33

Share with Your Family

Set out a small jar of oil. In Bible times, oil was poured onto the head of every new king in Israel. It symbolized God's special blessing and a pouring out of God's Spirit.

With oil on your fingertip, draw a cross on each person's forehead. Anoint and bless each other. (You might say, "I bless you in the name of the Father and the Son and the Holy Spirit.")

Pray together, asking Jesus to anoint you with His power to live the kind of life He wants you to live.

Bible Promises

"May the God of hope fill you with all joy and peace as you trust in him, so that you may overflow with hope by the power of the Holy Spirit."
Romans 15:13 (NIV)

"Is anyone among you sick? Let him call for the elders of the church, and let them pray over him, anointing him with oil in the name of the Lord." James 5:14

"I will pour My Spirit on your descendants, And My blessing on your offspring."
Isaiah 44:3

"I know that the Lord saves His anointed; He will answer him from His holy heaven with the saving strength of His right hand."
Psalm 20:6

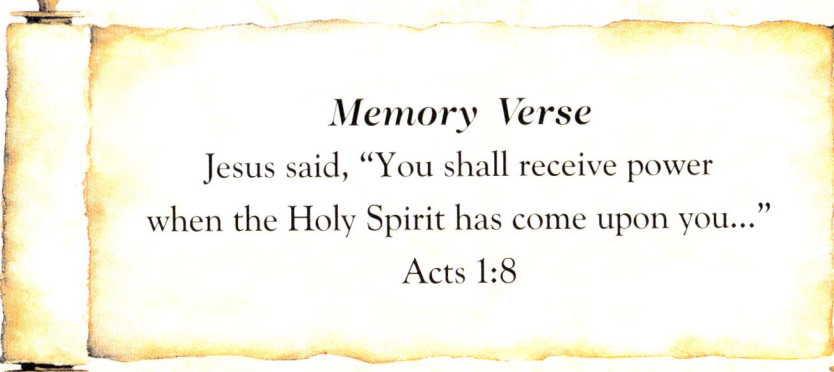

Memory Verse
Jesus said, "You shall receive power when the Holy Spirit has come upon you…"
Acts 1:8

"My cup runs over."

Inside every sheep pen, the shepherd stores a large stone jar of water. This jar of unglazed pottery keeps the water cool, even during the hot summer.

In the evening, the flock enters the sheep pen to settle down for the night. The shepherd dips a large cup into the water jar and brings out an overflowing drink for each sheep.

When a sheep becomes feverish, it sinks its nose into the cup all the way up to its eyes. The shepherd is not stingy with the water. The sheep drinks its fill.

After the flock lies down to sleep, their shepherd lies down in the open gateway of the sheep pen. No sheep can go out except across his body. No wolf can come into the sheep pen except across his body. When the shepherd guards the entrance to the pen, he becomes the door of protection for his sheep.

Ask Yourself

How is Jesus like the shepherd who becomes the door for his sheep?

What do you do at night before you fall asleep? Will you take time to talk with Jesus?

Do you thank Jesus for all His gifts? Especially those you don't deserve?

Jesus cares about everything in your life. Take time to be with Him and enjoy Him.

My Cup Runs Over

Jesus said, "...he who does not enter the sheepfold by the door, but climbs up some other way, the same is a thief and a robber. But he who enters by the door is the shepherd of the sheep.

"Most assuredly, I say to you, I am the door of the sheep. All who ever came before Me are thieves and robbers, but the sheep did not hear them.

"I am the door. If anyone enters by Me, he will be saved, and will go in and out and find pasture.

"I am the good shepherd...and I lay down My life for the sheep." John 10:1–2, 7–9, 14–15

Share with Your Family

Hide a tin of popcorn or trail mix in the house or the yard. Scatter clues. When found, share it while all of you describe three blessings for which you are thankful.

What are the greatest blessings Jesus gives you?

What happens when you think about things you *don't* have instead of thanking Jesus for all the blessings you *do* have?

What does it mean to you that Jesus is your Good Shepherd? Isn't this the greatest blessing of all?

Bible Promises

"Bless the Lord, O my soul,
And forget not all His benefits."
Psalm 103:2

"Every good gift and every perfect gift is from above,
and comes down from the Father of lights."
James 1:17

"May the God of hope fill you with all joy and peace
as you trust in him, so that you may overflow with hope
by the power of the Holy Spirit."
Romans 15:13 (NIV)

"How we praise God...who has blessed us with
every blessing in heaven because we belong to [Jesus]."
Ephesians 1:3 (TLB)

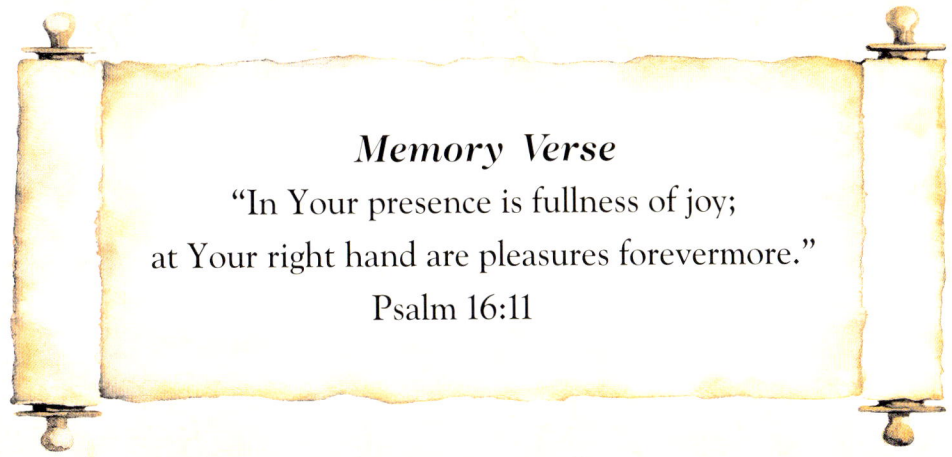

Memory Verse
"In Your presence is fullness of joy;
at Your right hand are pleasures forevermore."
Psalm 16:11

"Surely goodness and mercy shall follow me all the days of my life."

At the end of summer, it is time to leave the highland pastures, head back down the mountain, and pass through the dark valley again.

By now the sheep know their shepherd well. They trust him for their food, water, and protection. And from now on, they can trust him to take them over hard places and through hard times.

The shepherd is not only good to his sheep, he shows them *mercy*. He loves them even when they look or act unlovable.

Jesus, your Good Shepherd, knows how to take care of you. You can trust Him to work out every problem, every trouble, and every disaster for your good.

Hurray! What a joy to be one of *His* sheep. Jump, kick up your heels, and shout, *"Yes!* Jesus is so good to me. I will love Him and trust Him and do everything He says."

Ask Yourself

Are you happy that Jesus loves you?

Will you thank Him and trust Him even when things go wrong?

You can trust that Jesus' goodness and love is all around you—even when it doesn't look like it. Your Good Shepherd always turns bad into good for you.

Surely Goodness and Mercy Shall Follow Me All the Days of My Life

Jesus said, "Love your enemies, do good to those who hate you, bless those who curse you...Give to everyone who asks of you.

"If you do good to those who do good to you, what credit is that to you?

"But love your enemies, do good, and lend, hoping for nothing in return; and your reward will be great, and you will be sons of the Most High. For He is kind to the unthankful and evil.

"Therefore be merciful, just as your Father also is merciful."   Luke 6:27–28, 30, 33, 35–36

Share with Your Family

Hand out pencils and pieces of paper. Have each person write down five special love gifts from Jesus. (Let little ones draw pictures.)

Talk about people in the Bible who received God's goodness and mercy. (Read about Noah, Abraham, Moses, Daniel, King David, Peter, Paul, etc.)

Where do you see God's goodness and mercy in your life? When have you shown mercy and undeserved love to someone?

Bible Promises

"And we know that all things work together for good to those who love God, to those who are the called according to His purpose."
Romans 8:28

"Now to him who is able to do immeasurably more than all we ask or imagine... to him be glory..."
Ephesians 3:20–21 (NIV)

"The Lord is good to all,
And His tender mercies are over all His works."
Psalm 145:9

"The steadfast love of the Lord never ceases, his mercies never come to an end."
Lamentations 3:22 (RSV)

Memory Verse
"Oh, give thanks to the Lord, for He is good!
For His mercy endures forever."
Psalm 118:29

"And I will dwell in the house of the Lord forever."

The shepherd always leads his sheep back home for the long cold winter. The sheep want to stay close to their shepherd. They feel "at home" when they are with him. To arrive safely in the valley, they follow their shepherd and obey him all along the way. They look forward to being home and spending time with their shepherd.

Jesus, your Good Shepherd, leads you on the journey of *your* life. One day He will take you to the special home He's made ready just for you in heaven.

Heaven is the place of perfect love and peace. In heaven, joy and love last forever. No more tears, no more troubles, no more good-byes.

Can you imagine a home with no pain, no anger, no sadness, no arguments, and no death? How wonderful it will be to live with Jesus someday in heaven!

Ask Yourself

Do you look forward to living with Jesus forever?
Are you staying close to your Good Shepherd by reading the Bible, praying, and praising Him?
Do you trust His promise to take you to heaven? Remember, **Jesus** is the only way to heaven. So don't get lost! Follow Him.

And I Will Dwell in the House of the Lord Forever

Jesus said, "Let not your heart be troubled; you believe in God, believe also in Me. In My Father's house are many mansions; if it were not so, I would have told you. I go to prepare a place for you.

"And if I go and prepare a place for you, I will come again and receive you to Myself; that where I am, there you may be also." John 14:1–3

"Behold, I am coming quickly, and My reward is with Me,...I am the Alpha and the Omega, the Beginning and the End, the First and the Last."
Revelation 22:12–13

Share with Your Family

Talk about heaven—especially the things you look forward to the most.

How can you be sure that you will be in heaven?

What do you think Jesus is preparing in heaven?

Think of events on earth that come to an end—vacations, basketball games, parties, etc. What do you think *eternity* will be like?

Who is waiting for you in heaven?

Bible Promises

"And this is the promise
that He has promised us—eternal life."
1 John 2:25

Jesus said, "I am the resurrection and the life.
He who believes in Me, though he may die,
he shall live." John 11:25

"And God will wipe away every tear from their eyes;
there shall be no more death, nor sorrow,
nor crying. There shall be no more pain."
Revelation 21:4

Jesus said, "To him who overcomes, I will grant
to sit with Me on My throne, as I also overcame and
sat down with My Father on His throne."
Revelation 3:21

Memory Verse
Jesus said, "Be faithful until death,
and I will give you the crown of life."
Revelation 2:10

John wrote in the Book of Revelation:

"Now I saw a new heaven and a new earth, for the first heaven and the first earth had passed away....I heard a loud voice from heaven saying, 'Behold, the tabernacle of God is with men, and He will dwell with them, and they shall be His people. God Himself will be with them and be their God.'

"And God will wipe away every tear from their eyes; there shall be no more death, nor sorrow, nor crying. There shall be no more pain, for the former things have passed away....I saw no temple in it, for the Lord God Almighty and [Jesus] are its temple. The city had no need of the sun or of the moon to shine in it, for the glory of God illuminated it....And there shall be no more curse, but the throne of God and of [Jesus] shall be in it, and His servants shall serve Him. They shall see His face, and His name shall be on their foreheads. There shall be no night there. They need no lamp nor light of the sun, for the Lord God gives them light. And they shall reign forever and ever...

"Then [Jesus] said, 'And behold, I am coming quickly, and My reward is with Me, to give to every one according to his work. I am the Alpha and the Omega, the Beginning and the End, the First and the Last....Surely I am coming quickly.'"

Revelation 21:1—22:20

Celebrate Your Good Shepherd

When you finish reading this book, plan a special celebration. Let everyone help prepare a buffet supper. Place a cross in the center of your table. Eat by candlelight. Set out an extra unlit candle at each person's place.

Take time at the end of supper to say the 23rd Psalm together. Memorize it.

How can you be sure Jesus cares for you and will help you through every difficulty? *(Look at the cross.)*

Take turns expressing what it means to know that Jesus is your Good Shepherd.

After supper, have people rededicate their lives to Jesus. Have them light their candle from the candles in the center of the table.

Then all of you light your candles. In the glow that reminds you that Jesus called Himself "The Light of the World," pray for one another. Ask Jesus to bless you and make you a blessing to others.

How to Receive Jesus as Your Savior and Good Shepherd

You are loved.
"For God so loved the world that He gave His only begotten Son, that whoever believes in Him should not perish but have everlasting life."
John 3:16

You need a Savior.
"...for all have sinned and fall short of the glory of God..."
Romans 3:23

Jesus died for you.
Jesus said, "I am the good shepherd. The good shepherd gives his life for the sheep." John 10:11

Jesus invites you to receive Him.
"Behold, I stand at the door and knock. If anyones hears My voice and opens the door, I will come in to him..."
Revelation 3:20

Open your heart to Jesus. Pray a prayer like this:
Thank You, Jesus, for dying on the cross for me.
Forgive all I've done wrong. Come into my heart.
Thank You for loving and forgiving me.
Thank You for promising me a home in heaven.
Help me live for you. Amen.

Trust that you are forgiven.
"If we confess our sins, He is faithful and just
to forgive us our sins…" 1 John 1:9

You can be sure of the gift of eternal life.
"…if you confess with your mouth the Lord Jesus and believe
in your heart that God has raised Him from the dead,
you will be saved." Romans 10:9